THE HOLOCAUST

**A record of the destruction of Jewish life in Europe
during the dark years of Nazi rule**

MAPS AND PHOTOGRAPHS BY MARTIN GILBERT

 **Hill and Wang • New York**
A division of Farrar, Straus and Giroux

OTHER ATLASES BY MARTIN GILBERT

Jewish History Atlas
The Arab-Israeli Conflict: Its History in Maps
Recent History Atlas, 1870–1970
British World History Atlas from Earliest Times to the Present Day
First World War Atlas

Published simultaneously in Canada by McGraw-Hill Ryerson Ltd., Toronto
Second printing, 1979
Printed in the United States of America
Library of Congress catalog card number 79-84287

PREFACE

The fate of the Jews of Europe in the Nazi era was one of the greatest horrors of human history. It has recently become a subject of dispute and controversy. Tragically, for those millions of innocent men, women and children who were murdered, the dispute is an insult to their memory. Their lives are gone. So too is the life of which they were a part: the Jewish cultural, religious and communal heritage which spanned two thousand years of European history.

In this atlas, I have tried to tell something of the story of those whose lives were destroyed. No map, and no photograph, can convey more than the tiniest fragment of the torment and tortures which so many people suffered, some of them so young, some old and frail, all of them normal human beings, who had committed no crime. They perished solely because they were Jews; because they were the children of their parents; because evil men triumphed over sanity and civilized human feelings.

The terrible story outlined in these pages took place within the last forty years. It cannot be denied, or ignored, unless we wish to deny our own past.

Cover Picture – Plate 1: Two starving Jewish children in the Warsaw Ghetto, recorded by a German photographer. Born into an ordinary Jewish family, they, and the two little boys on page i, were among the one and a half *million* child victims of The Holocaust.

Plate 2 (page i): In the Warsaw Ghetto: 'Children at mealtime.' After living for two years in the Ghetto, with so little food that several thousand died of starvation, more than 100,000 Jewish children were deported to the death camp at Treblinka, and murdered there.

ACKNOWLEDGEMENTS

The maps and photographs in this atlas are drawn from materials which I have been collecting for some time, in the hope eventually of publishing a comprehensive illustrated atlas of The Holocaust, region by region and community by community. Meanwhile, I am grateful to Martin Savitt and Paul Shaw, of the Board of Deputies of British Jews, for suggesting that I should put some of my materials in this shortened form, and for their important help in initiating this project, guiding it, and making its realisation possible.

My particular thanks are due to Terry Bicknell, the British cartographer, who has prepared each of the twenty-three maps, and Zev Radovan of Jerusalem and Gerry Moeran of Oxford, who prepared the photographic prints, many of them taken from faded or damaged originals.

The staffs of the Wiener Library, London; and of Yad Vashem, Jerusalem have both been extremely helpful in providing materials and answering questions, both for this atlas, and for the larger project. I should also like to thank Reuben Ainsztein, Hugo Gryn and Martin Sieff for their help on specific points, and for their encouragement.

Beginning on page 54, I have listed those books and other sources on which I have drawn for the facts shown on the twenty-three maps. On page 56 I have listed the sources for each of the sixty illustrations.

I should welcome both suggestions and amendments for future editions of this atlas.

Martin Gilbert
Merton College
Oxford
27 February 1978

LIST OF MAPS

Plate 3: The decorated interior of an eastern European synagogue. Tens of thousands of such synagogues, many of them several hundred years old, were destroyed by the Nazis during the second world war, while at the same time all their precious articles, such as silver candlesticks and other decorations were seized, and melted down or sold to provide money for the German war machine.

1

TWO THOUSAND YEARS OF JEWISH LIFE IN EUROPE

This map shows the age of the principal European Jewish communities in 1939. It was the Jewish communities shown here - their culture, their customs, and their deep local roots - which the Nazis sought utterly to destroy in the second world war.

0   miles   200
0   km   200

NORWAY
88 YEARS

North Sea

ESTONIA
600 YEARS

LATVIA
400 YEARS

DENMARK
317 YEARS

HOLLAND
800 YEARS

LITHUANIA
600 YEARS

WHITE RUSSIA
550 YEARS

BELGIUM
700 YEARS

GERMANY
1,618 YEARS

POLAND
850 YEARS

UKRAINE
822 YEARS

LUXEMBOURG
653 YEARS

CZECHOSLOVAKIA
1,000 YEARS

CRIMEA
1,900 YEARS

FRANCE
1,936 YEARS

HUNGARY
1,900 YEARS

RUMANIA
1,800 YEARS

AUSTRIA
1,030 YEARS

YUGOSLAVIA
1,000 YEARS

Adriatic Sea

ITALY
2,100 YEARS

Black Sea

GREECE
2,239 YEARS

Most of the Jewish communities of Europe had come into existence hundreds of years *before* the founding of the States of which they were to become a part. Others had subsequently been destroyed by expulsion and persecution in the middle ages - but had then been refounded a second, a third, and even a fourth time. The Jews of Germany had already been living continuously in different parts of Germany for more than 1,500 years when the German Empire was established in 1870, the year of German unity under Bismarck.

The age, by 1939, of the Jewish communities of Europe.

—·—· The European frontiers of 1937.

© Martin Gilbert 1978

Map 1

Plate 4: This synagogue in eastern Europe was typical of tens of thousand of synagogues, large and small, which for centuries had served as the hub of Jewish communal and religious life. Almost all of them were destroyed during the Second World War, together with the communities which they served.

A THOUSAND YEARS OF JEWISH CULTURE AND COMMUNAL LIFE

Between 1000 AD and 1939 the Jews of Europe, despite constant persecution, maintained unbroken their traditional community and family life, including observance of the Holy-days, the keeping of the Sabbath, communal self-help, charity, and the strong encouragement of learning and scholarship, and a belief in the common destiny of the Jewish people, to survive *as a people*.

miles 150
km 100

North Sea

Baltic Sea

Copenhagen 1606

Vitebsk · Lyubavichi
Lyady

Vilna ◉

Hamburg 1586

Zabludow

Karlin

Berlin 1798

Gur

Mezhirech

Amsterdam 1526

Erfurt 1400

Padom

Lublin 1571

Polonnoye

Antwerp 1523

Pinczow

Belz

Berdichev

Mainz 1000 AD 1220 1250 1381

Prague 1512

Cracow 1592

Lvov 1788

Medzhibozh

Paris 1508

Worms 1196

Gorodenka

Bratslav

Troyes 1150-1160

Munkacs

Czernowitz

Satmar

Odessa ◉

Bologna 1416

Venice 1516

Not only did the Nazis seek to eliminate the cultural, communal, and spiritual life of European Jewry; they also seized, expropriated, or destroyed the homes, shops, property, economic assets, financial savings and material belongings of more than six million Jews, the inheritance of over a thousand years of effort, achievement and creativity.

Soncino 1483

Avignon 1765

Genoa 1516

Nice 1773

Florence 1428

Adriatic Sea

Mediterranean Sea

Black Sea

1486 Rome 1469

Salonica 1513

Corfu 1642

☆ Some of the Rabbinical Councils between 1000 AD and 1642 which laid down the laws for Jewish communal life (with their dates).

● Hebrew printing presses, publishing Hebrew books with the date of their first recorded publications.

○ Important printings of Jewish prayer books, published between 1486 and 1798.

◉ The first weekly newspapers printed in Hebrew, both in 1860.

✤ Some of the centres of Hassidism, a Jewish popular religious movement which brought together charismatic leadership, religious enthusiasm, and a closely-knit social life. Founded in the 1730s, Hassidism flourished throughout eastern Europe for two hundred years. Despite the Nazi destruction of the great Hassidic centres, and the brutal murder of tens of thousands of its followers, Hassidism continues to flourish in the United States, Israel, and Britain.

© Martin Gilbert 1978

4

Map 2

Plate 5: The interior of the synagogue at Przemysl, a photograph taken at the turn of the century. At the outbreak of war in 1939 there were some 20,000 Jews in Przemysl. Only 250 survived the executions and death-camp deportations. A group of young Jews who managed to escape from the city in April 1943, intent on joining the partisans, were captured by German troops, and murdered.

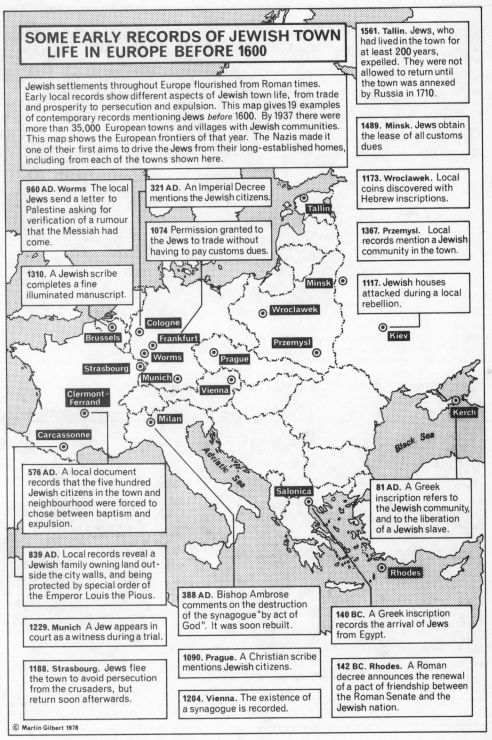

SOME EARLY RECORDS OF JEWISH TOWN LIFE IN EUROPE BEFORE 1600

Jewish settlements throughout Europe flourished from Roman times. Early local records show different aspects of Jewish town life, from trade and prosperity to persecution and expulsion. This map gives 19 examples of contemporary records mentioning Jews *before* 1600. By 1937 there were more than 35,000 European towns and villages with Jewish communities. This map shows the European frontiers of that year. The Nazis made it one of their first aims to drive the Jews from their long-established homes, including from each of the towns shown here.

1561. Tallin. Jews, who had lived in the town for at least 200 years, expelled. They were not allowed to return until the town was annexed by Russia in 1710.

1489. Minsk. Jews obtain the lease of all customs dues

1173. Wroclawek. Local coins discovered with Hebrew inscriptions.

1367. Przemysl. Local records mention a Jewish community in the town.

1117. Jewish houses attacked during a local rebellion.

960 AD. Worms The local Jews send a letter to Palestine asking for verification of a rumour that the Messiah had come.

321 AD. An Imperial Decree mentions the Jewish citizens.

1074 Permission granted to the Jews to trade without having to pay customs dues.

1310. A Jewish scribe completes a fine illuminated manuscript.

576 AD. A local document records that the five hundred Jewish citizens in the town and neighbourhood were forced to chose between baptism and expulsion.

839 AD. Local records reveal a Jewish family owning land outside the city walls, and being protected by special order of the Emperor Louis the Pious.

1229. Munich A Jew appears in court as a witness during a trial.

1188. Strasbourg. Jews flee the town to avoid persecution from the crusaders, but return soon afterwards.

388 AD. Bishop Ambrose comments on the destruction of the synagogue "by act of God". It was soon rebuilt.

1090. Prague. A Christian scribe mentions Jewish citizens.

1204. Vienna. The existence of a synagogue is recorded.

81 AD. A Greek inscription refers to the Jewish community, and to the liberation of a Jewish slave.

140 BC. A Greek inscription records the arrival of Jews from Egypt.

142 BC. Rhodes. A Roman decree announces the renewal of a pact of friendship between the Roman Senate and the Jewish nation.

Map labels: Tallin, Minsk, Wroclawek, Przemysl, Kiev, Cologne, Frankfurt, Brussels, Worms, Prague, Strasbourg, Munich, Vienna, Clermont-Ferrand, Milan, Carcassonne, Kerch, Black Sea, Adriatic Sea, Salonica, Rhodes

© Martin Gilbert 1978

Map 3

Plate 6: A scene in the Lodz Ghetto. Jews from Germany, Austria and Czechoslovakia were deported to Lodz, and forced to live, with meagre rations and in grossly overcrowded quarters, with the 200,000 local Jewish citizens. Terror raids, disease and deportations led to more than 100,000 deaths by October 1942. In June 1944 the Nazis began the systematic murder of all survivors; by September 1944 more than 75,000 of the ghetto's inhabitants had been deported to Auschwitz and murdered.

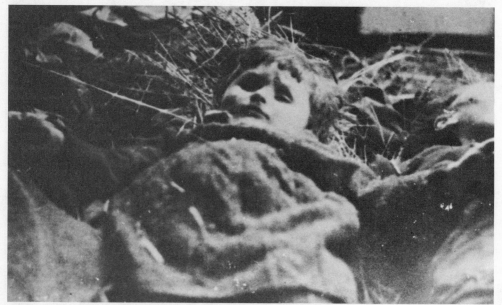

Plate 7: A four year old boy, Tolka Zhitomir, murdered by the Nazis in Bialystok with several hundred other children on 17 February 1945, as the Soviet liberation forces approached the city. Of the 50,000 Jews living in Bialystok in 1939, less than 2,000 survived the exterminations and death-camp deportations of 1941 to 1944.

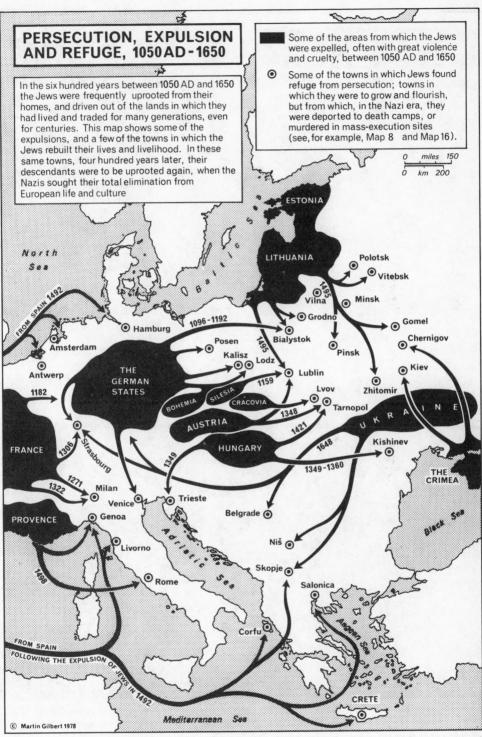

PERSECUTION, EXPULSION AND REFUGE, 1050 AD – 1650

In the six hundred years between 1050 AD and 1650 the Jews were frequently uprooted from their homes, and driven out of the lands in which they had lived and traded for many generations, even for centuries. This map shows some of the expulsions, and a few of the towns in which the Jews rebuilt their lives and livelihood. In these same towns, four hundred years later, their descendants were to be uprooted again, when the Nazis sought their total elimination from European life and culture

■ Some of the areas from which the Jews were expelled, often with great violence and cruelty, between 1050 AD and 1650

⊙ Some of the towns in which Jews found refuge from persecution; towns in which they were to grow and flourish, but from which, in the Nazi era, they were deported to death camps, or murdered in mass-execution sites (see, for example, Map 8 and Map 16).

0   miles   150
0   km   200

North Sea

Baltic Sea

ESTONIA

LITHUANIA

FROM SPAIN 1492

Polotsk
Vitebsk
1495
Vilna
Minsk
Grodno
Gomel
Chernigov
Kiev
Hamburg
1096-1192
Posen
1495
Bialystok
Pinsk
Zhitomir
Amsterdam
Kalisz
Lodz
Lublin
Antwerp
THE GERMAN STATES
1182
Lvov
Tarnopol
1159
BOHEMIA
SILESIA
CRACOVIA
1348
UKRAINE
1306
Strasbourg
AUSTRIA
1421
FRANCE
HUNGARY
1648
Kishinev
1349
1349-1360
THE CRIMEA
1271
Milan
1322
Venice
Trieste
Belgrade
PROVENCE
Genoa
Niš
Black Sea
1498
Livorno
Adriatic Sea
Skopje
Rome
Salonica
Aegean Sea
FROM SPAIN
FOLLOWING THE EXPULSION OF JEWS IN 1492
Corfu
CRETE
© Martin Gilbert 1978
Mediterranean Sea

8

Map 4

Plate 8: A Jewish woman laments the destruction of her home during the Kishinev pogrom of 1903.

Plate 9: Four Ukrainian Cossacks pose with the corpses of Jews whom they have just murdered. The photograph is dated 10 August 1919. The dead Jews have been wrapped in their prayer shawls.

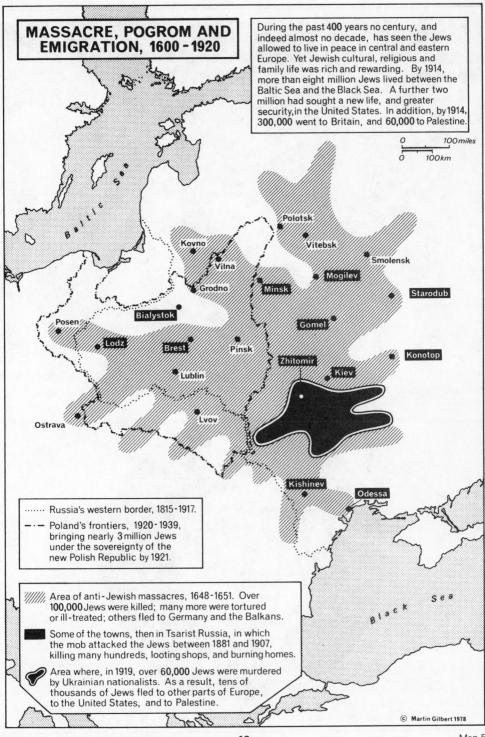

MASSACRE, POGROM AND EMIGRATION, 1600 – 1920

During the past 400 years no century, and indeed almost no decade, has seen the Jews allowed to live in peace in central and eastern Europe. Yet Jewish cultural, religious and family life was rich and rewarding. By 1914, more than eight million Jews lived between the Baltic Sea and the Black Sea. A further two million had sought a new life, and greater security, in the United States. In addition, by 1914, 300,000 went to Britain, and 60,000 to Palestine.

0   100 miles
0   100 km

Baltic Sea

Polotsk
Kovno
Vitebsk
Vilna
Smolensk
Grodno
Mogilev
Minsk
Starodub
Bialystok
Posen
Gomel
Lodz
Brest
Pinsk
Konotop
Zhitomir
Lublin
Kiev
Ostrava
Lvov
Kishinev
Odessa

Black Sea

.... Russia's western border, 1815 - 1917.

—··— Poland's frontiers, 1920 - 1939, bringing nearly 3 million Jews under the sovereignty of the new Polish Republic by 1921.

▨ Area of anti-Jewish massacres, 1648-1651. Over 100,000 Jews were killed; many more were tortured or ill-treated; others fled to Germany and the Balkans.

■ Some of the towns, then in Tsarist Russia, in which the mob attacked the Jews between 1881 and 1907, killing many hundreds, looting shops, and burning homes.

Area where, in 1919, over 60,000 Jews were murdered by Ukrainian nationalists. As a result, tens of thousands of Jews fled to other parts of Europe, to the United States, and to Palestine.

© Martin Gilbert 1978

Map 5

Plate 10: Germany, 10 May 1933. The public burning of books by Jewish authors. Young Nazis parade around the fire.

Plate 11: A Nazi beer mat. Its message reads: 'Whoever buys from a Jew is a traitor to his people'.

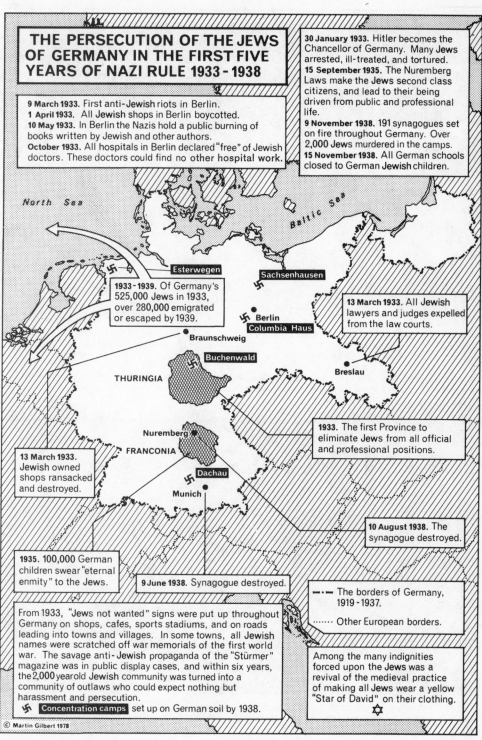

THE PERSECUTION OF THE JEWS OF GERMANY IN THE FIRST FIVE YEARS OF NAZI RULE 1933-1938

9 March 1933. First anti-Jewish riots in Berlin.
1 April 1933. All Jewish shops in Berlin boycotted.
10 May 1933. In Berlin the Nazis hold a public burning of books written by Jewish and other authors.
October 1933. All hospitals in Berlin declared "free" of Jewish doctors. These doctors could find no other hospital work.

30 January 1933. Hitler becomes the Chancellor of Germany. Many Jews arrested, ill-treated, and tortured.
15 September 1935. The Nuremberg Laws make the Jews second class citizens, and lead to their being driven from public and professional life.
9 November 1938. 191 synagogues set on fire throughout Germany. Over 2,000 Jews murdered in the camps.
15 November 1938. All German schools closed to German Jewish children.

North Sea

Baltic Sea

Esterwegen

Sachsenhausen

1933-1939. Of Germany's 525,000 Jews in 1933, over 280,000 emigrated or escaped by 1939.

Berlin
Columbia Haus

13 March 1933. All Jewish lawyers and judges expelled from the law courts.

Braunschweig

Buchenwald

THURINGIA

Breslau

1933. The first Province to eliminate Jews from all official and professional positions.

Nuremberg

FRANCONIA

13 March 1933. Jewish owned shops ransacked and destroyed.

Dachau

Munich

10 August 1938. The synagogue destroyed.

1935. 100,000 German children swear "eternal enmity" to the Jews.

9 June 1938. Synagogue destroyed.

— · — The borders of Germany, 1919-1937.

······ Other European borders.

From 1933, "Jews not wanted" signs were put up throughout Germany on shops, cafes, sports stadiums, and on roads leading into towns and villages. In some towns, all Jewish names were scratched off war memorials of the first world war. The savage anti-Jewish propaganda of the "Stürmer" magazine was in public display cases, and within six years, the 2,000 year old Jewish community was turned into a community of outlaws who could expect nothing but harassment and persecution.

Concentration camps set up on German soil by 1938.

Among the many indignities forced upon the Jews was a revival of the medieval practice of making all Jews wear a yellow "Star of David" on their clothing.

© Martin Gilbert 1978

12

Map 6

Plate 12: German soldiers execute Jews. At the Wannsee Conference, several leading Nazis, including Adolf Eichmann, agreed on what they called 'the final solution of the Jewish question'. All Jews who were capable of work were to be eliminated by means of forced labour. Those who were, according to the official minutes of the meeting, 'not capable of work', would be 'dealt with appropriately'.
To carry out this 'final solution', the meeting decided, Europe was to be 'combed from east to west'. Men and women were to be separated, so that there would be no more Jewish children.

Plate 13: One of the crematorium ovens at Dachau concentration camp. This photograph was taken on 2 May 1945 by an American sergeant who was among the first Allied troops to enter the camp at the liberation.

GERMAN OFFICIAL PLANS FOR THE "FINAL SOLUTION", 20 JANUARY 1942

The number of Jews mentioned at the Wannsee Conference, country by country and area by area, for eventual deportation, and subsequent death. More than 14 million people were thus marked out for death.

One of the macabre features of the numerical list of the Jews submitted to the Wannsee Conference was the fact that no figure was given for the Jews of Estonia, merely a brief note that Estonia was 'Free of Jews'. This was true; the 1,000 Estonian Jews who had come under German rule in October 1941 had all been murdered during the three months before the Wannsee Conference.

ESTONIA "Free of Jews"

USSR 5 million

NORWAY 1,300

LATVIA 3,500

LITHUANIA 34,000

DENMARK 5,600

HOLLAND 160,800

BIALYSTOK DISTRICT 400,000

WHITE RUSSIA 446,484

BELGIUM 43,000

Wannsee
GERMANY 131,800 ● Berlin

Chelmno

GENERAL GOVERNM.NT 2,284,000

EASTERN TERRITORIES 420,000

88,000

UKRAINE 2,994,684

FRANCE OCCUPIED ZONE 165,000

BOHEMIA AND MORAVIA 74,200

SLOVAKIA

HUNGARY 742,800

FRANCE UNOCCUPIED ZONE 700,000

AUSTRIA 43,700

CROATIA 40,000

10,000

SERBIA

RUMANIA 342,000

ITALY 58,000

ALBANIA 200

BULGARIA

48,000

0   miles   200
0   km   300

GREECE 69,600

In December 1941, a month *before* the Wannsee Conference, the first Nazi extermination camp had already come into operation, at Chelmno, responsible for the mass-murder of Jews, Gypsies, and Soviet prisoners-of-war. After passing through corridors marked 'To the showers' and 'To the doctor', the victims were forced into a large truck which was in fact a gas-chamber, where they were killed within a few minutes. By the end of 1944 more than 360,000 Jews had been murdered in Chelmno alone.

The Wannsee Conference also specified the number of Jews in *unconquered* countries for eventual destruction, including **330,000** from Britain, **18,000** from Switzerland, **6,000** from Spain and **4,000** from Ireland.

© Martin Gilbert 1978

Map 7

Plate 14: At Mauthausen concentration camp the American liberation forces discovered this mound of murdered Jews, whom the Nazis had not had time to bury or to burn before the arrival of the Allies. In this camp alone more than 122,000 prisoners were murdered, including Jews — who were often singled out for especially cruel tortures — Russian prisoners of war, Gypsies, and prominent non-Jews from all over German-occupied Europe.

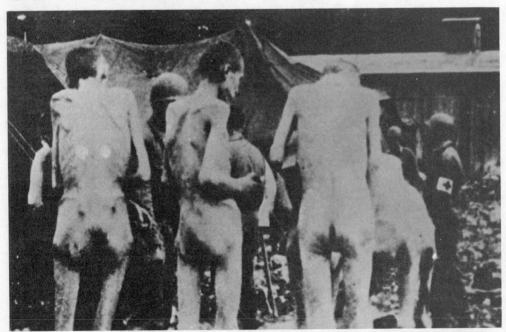

Plate 15: Survivors at Mauthausen, naked and starving, are given their first proper meal for months, if not years, by American medical and Red Cross personnel.

THE CONCENTRATION CAMPS

Between 1939 and 1945, six million unarmed and innocent Jewish civilians - men, women, children and babies - were murdered in Nazi-controlled Europe, as part of a deliberate policy to destroy all traces of Jewish life and culture. As many as two million of these were killed in their own towns and villages, some confined in ghettoes where death by slow starvation was a deliberate Nazi policy, others taken to be shot at mass-murder sites near where they lived. The remaining four million Jews were forced from their homes and taken by train to distant concentration camps, where they were murdered by being worked to death, starved to death, beaten to death, shot, or gassed.

Vaivara

Klooga
ESTONIA

LATVIA

LITHUANIA

North Sea

U S S R

Stutthof

Neuengamme   Ravensbrück

Bergen-Belsen   Sachsenhausen   Chelmno   Treblinka

P O L A N D

Mittelbau Dora   Gross Rosen   Sobibor

Buchenwald   Auschwitz   Maidanek

G E R M A N Y   Belzec

Flossenberg   C Z E C H O S L O V A K I A   Plaszow

Natzweiler

FRANCE   Dachau

Mauthausen

A U S T R I A   H U N G A R Y   RUMANIA

Gospič   Jasenovac

Y U G O S L A V I A   Sajmište

I T A L Y

Adriatic Sea

Among the hundreds of thousands of *non*-Jews sent by the Nazis to concentration camps were anti-Nazis, Jehovah's Witnesses, homosexuals, the mentally ill, and the chronically sick. In addition, more than 250,000 Gypsies were murdered, in a Nazi attempt to eliminate Gypsies as well as Jews from the map of Europe.

Auschwitz concentration camp in which more than 2 *million* people were murdered between 1941 and 1944, including Jews, Gypsies, and Soviet prisoners-of-war.

Camps set up solely for the murder of Jews.

Other camps in which Jews and non-Jews were put to forced labour, starved, tortured, and murdered in conditions of the worst imaginable cruelty. Most of these camps had "satellite" labour camps nearby.

In many of the camps shown here so-called "medical" experiments were carried out, without anaesthetics, solely to satisfy the curiosity and sadism of the doctors. Hundreds of otherwise healthy "patients" were tortured and murdered during these experiments.

0   100 miles
0   100 km

© Martin Gilbert 1978

Plate 16: Dachau concentration camp. A photograph taken on 29 April 1945, the day on which the camp was liberated by American troops. By the day of the liberation, more than 40,000 people had been murdered in Dachau, of whom over 80% were Jews.

Plate 17: Plaszow labour camp. Women prisoners pulling heavy trucks. As many as 20,000 Jews were employed here at any one time, mainly in metalwork, glasswork, clothing and brushmaking for German firms. Workers were shot on the smallest pretext. In all, more than 9,000 workers died from exhaustion, or were executed.

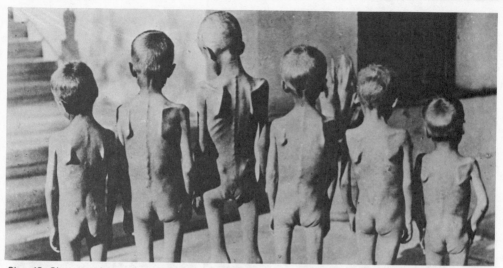

Plate 18: Six young boys, photographed in a concentration camp in Yugoslavia run by local fascists. At the liberation, the several hundred young boys found still alive in the camp had lost more than 60% of their normal weight. Most of them died within a few weeks, despite the care with which they were tended by the liberation forces.

Plate 19: Senator Alben W. Barkley of Kentucky, USA, visits Buchenwald concentration camp, and sees the corpses of the victims. This photograph was taken on 24 April 1945. Of the 238,380 prisoners registered in the camp between 1937 and 1945, a total of 56,549 had died of starvation, or been brutally murdered.

Plate 20: Poland, 1942. Seven Polish civilians are hanged publicly by the Germans, who announced officially that for every German shot by partisans they would kill one hundred Polish civilians as reprisals.

Plate 21: Russia, 1943. A German officer and his men pause during anti-partisan operations in Russia. As well as fighting the partisan units, these German troops also destroyed whole villages, and murdered innocent civilians throughout their areas of operations.

NON-JEWISH VICTIMS OF NAZI RULE

Twenty-six of many thousands of Nazi reprisal and murder actions against unarmed *non-Jews*, with the approximate number murdered in each massacre.

Countries in each of which more than a *million* non-Jewish civilians died as a result of deliberate Nazi brutality.

In all occupied lands, the Nazis carried out large-scale reprisals against completely innocent and unarmed civilians, whenever a single German soldier was killed by partisans, or even when German property was attacked. In mass-murder actions against non-Jews, they also massacred 2 *million* unarmed Soviet prisoners-of-war, 1 *million* Soviet civilians, more than 1 *million* Polish civilians, and 1½ *million* Yugoslav civilians. In May 1940, at two villages near Dunkirk, a total of 170 *disarmed* British prisoners-of-war were murdered in cold blood. In June 1944, at three villages near Caen, 70 *disarmed* Canadian prisoners-of-war were likewise murdered, by German S.S. troops.

North Sea

Baltic Sea

Burashevo 350

U.S.S.R

Jeglava 700

Mikulino 275

Baranowicze 1,000

English Channel

Holland 7 March 1945 400

Prague 860

Zinyany 484

Gorodets 434

GERMANY

POLAND

Borow 300

Ala 1,758

Dunkirk 170

Caen 70

FRANCE

Lidice 250

CZECHOSLOVAKIA

Brno 395

Zamosc 200

Studenets 402

AUSTRIA

HUNGARY

Oradour-sur-Glane 642

ITALY

YUGOSLAVIA

Adriatic Sea

RUMANIA

Belgrade 4,750

Kragujevac 7,253

Black Sea

Kraljevo 1,700

BULGARIA

Mediterranean Sea

Rome 335

GREECE

Distomon 270

Kalvrithia 50

Athens 200

0   miles   200
0   km   150

Klissura 233

CRETE

Kastelli 200

In each of the actions shown here, unarmed men, women and children, almost all non-Jews, were chosen as the victims of Nazi hatred and vengeance. Many of those killed were beaten to death by blows of rifle butts, burned to death after petrol had been poured over them and ignited *while they were still alive,* or stripped naked and then shot. Those murdered at Klissura included 50 children under ten years of age. At Mikulino, all those killed were women patients in a mental hospital. In the Ardeatine caves in Rome, 253 Catholics and 70 Jews were murdered, among them many shopkeepers, students, lawyers and peddlers.

An estimated 32,000 German civilians were executed between 1933 and 1945 for so-called "political" offences. Those killed included Conservatives, Socialists, Communists, Catholics, Protestants, writers, journalists and teachers. All over Europe, non-Jews who were discovered sheltering Jews were also shot.

© Martin Gilbert 1978

Map 9

Plate 22: A Gypsy woman prisoner, photographed by the German authorities at Auschwitz, together with the number tattooed on her arm, the letter 'Z' denoting Gypsy woman (in German, *Zigeunerin*).

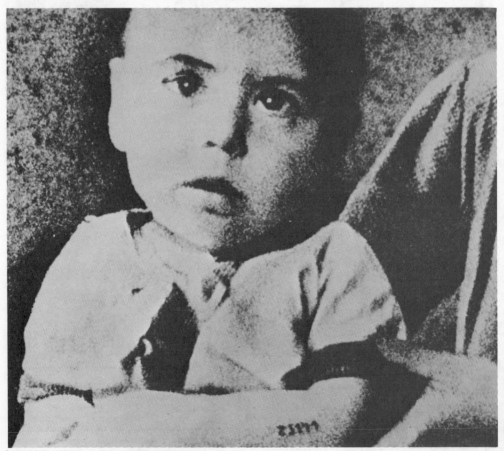

Plate 23: A Gypsy child, a survivor of Auschwitz, with her tattoo number on her arm.

21

THE FATE OF THE GYPSIES UNDER NAZI RULE

| 0 | miles | 200 |
| 0 | km | 150 |

In 1939 there were more than 700,000 gypsies living in Europe. At least 200,000 of them were murdered by the Nazis, as part of a deliberate policy aimed at "ridding" Europe of both its gypsies and its Jews.
A gypsy was defined by the Nazis as a person with at least two gypsy great-great-grandparents.

卐   Mass murder sites where gypsies as well as Jews were slaughtered.

⊙   Camps at which gypsies were forcibly sterilized.

卐   Concentration camps in which gypsies are known to have been murdered.

100,000   Number of gypsies in 1939, country by country.

▬   Number of gypsies murdered between 1942 and 1945: the Serbian figure is a minimum estimate.

GERMANY *20,000* 15,000

ESTONIA *1,000* 1,000

HOLLAND *500* 500

LATVIA *5,000* 2,500

LITHUANIA *1,000* 1,000

BELGIUM *600* 500

U.S.S.R.

Valogne

Bergen-Belsen

Treblinka

Dusseldorf

Gross Rosen

Chelmno

Sobibor

WESTERN U.S.S.R. *42,000* 30,000

Buchenwald

Maidanek

Belzec

Babi Yar

LUXEMBOURG *200* 200

Natzweiler

BOHEMIA *13,000* 6,500

Auschwitz

POLAND *50,000* 35,000

Dachau

AUSTRIA *11,200* 6,500

Nikolaev

FRANCE *40,000* 15,000

HUNGARY *100,000* 28,000

SLOVAKIA *80,000* 1,000

Simferopol

ITALY *25,000* 1,000

Zemun

RUMANIA *300,000* 36,000

CROATIA *28,500* 28,000

Black Sea

SERBIA *60,000* 12,000

By 1939 many German and Austrian gypsies had been sent to Buchenwald and Dachau. In 1940 all surviving German gypsies were deported to Poland, and forced to live in special sections set aside for them in the Ghettoes being established for Jews. Several thousand Serbian gypsies were murdered during German "field operations" in 1941, and many Crimean and Ukrainian gypsies were killed in January 1942 at mass-murder sites intended primarily for Jews. On 16 December 1942 a Nazi decree ordered gypsies from all over Europe to be deported to Auschwitz, where 16,000 were murdered on arrival at the camp.

"In Europe, generally only Jews and Gypsies are of foreign blood". **OFFICIAL GERMAN COMMENTARY ON THE NUREMBERG LAWS, 1935**

© Martin Gilbert 1978

22   Map 10

Plate 24: Photograph of a Jewish woman, taken during the festival of Hanukkah, in a cellar in Amsterdam in 1942. It was her last Hannuka celebration, for within a year she had been seized by the Gestapo and deported to Sobibor concentration camp, where she was murdered. Of the 34,000 Dutch Jews deported to Sobibor *only nineteen survived.*

Plate 25: French Jews arriving at Auschwitz. Many of them were little children who were taken straight to the gas chambers.

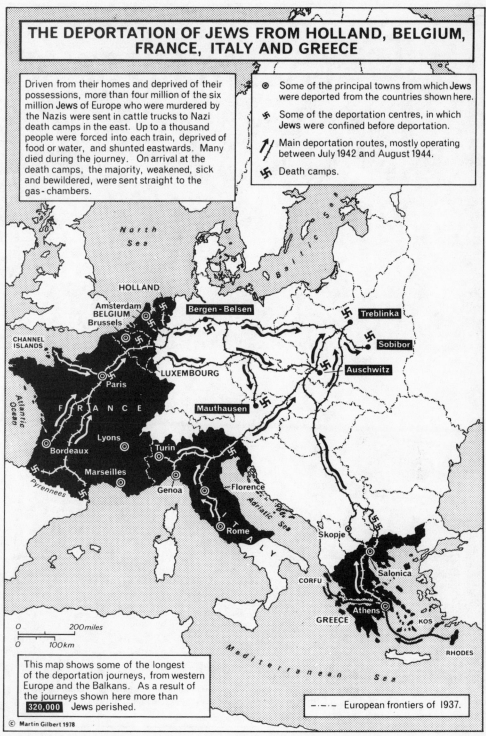

THE DEPORTATION OF JEWS FROM HOLLAND, BELGIUM, FRANCE, ITALY AND GREECE

Driven from their homes and deprived of their possessions, more than four million of the six million Jews of Europe who were murdered by the Nazis were sent in cattle trucks to Nazi death camps in the east. Up to a thousand people were forced into each train, deprived of food or water, and shunted eastwards. Many died during the journey. On arrival at the death camps, the majority, weakened, sick and bewildered, were sent straight to the gas-chambers.

⊙   Some of the principal towns from which **Jews** were deported from the countries shown here.

卐   Some of the deportation centres, in which **Jews** were confined before deportation.

⇑   Main deportation routes, mostly operating between July 1942 and August 1944.

卐   Death camps.

North Sea

Baltic Sea

HOLLAND

Amsterdam
BELGIUM
Brussels

Bergen - Belsen

Treblinka

CHANNEL ISLANDS

Sobibor

LUXEMBOURG

Auschwitz

Paris

F R A N C E

Mauthausen

Atlantic Ocean

Lyons

Bordeaux

Turin

Marseilles

Genoa

Florence

Pyrenees

Adriatic Sea

Rome

I T A L Y

Skopje

Salonica

CORFU

Athens

GREECE

KOS

RHODES

Mediterranean Sea

0   200 miles

0   100 km

This map shows some of the longest of the deportation journeys, from western Europe and the Balkans. As a result of the journeys shown here more than **320,000** Jews perished.

—·—·— European frontiers of 1937.

© Martin Gilbert 1978

Plate 26: A German road sign at the entrance to a village. It reads: 'We want no Jews. The Jews are our misfortune'.

Plate 27: Another German road sign: 'Jews are not wanted in this locality'. Both photographs were taken in the autumn of 1935 by a Dutch motor-cyclist, on the main road between the Dutch frontier, Hanover and Berlin.

Plate 28: The start of a terrible journey. Polish-born Jews, expelled from Germany at the end of October 1938, forced to live in stables at Zbaszyn, on the Polish-German frontier. In all, 15,000 Jews were expelled within 48 hours, unable to take with them more than the most meagre possessions, a small sack, a handbag or a briefcase. Finally admitted by Poland, within a year these refugees came once more under Nazi rule.

THE DESPERATE SEARCH FOR A COUNTRY OF REFUGE 1933-1945

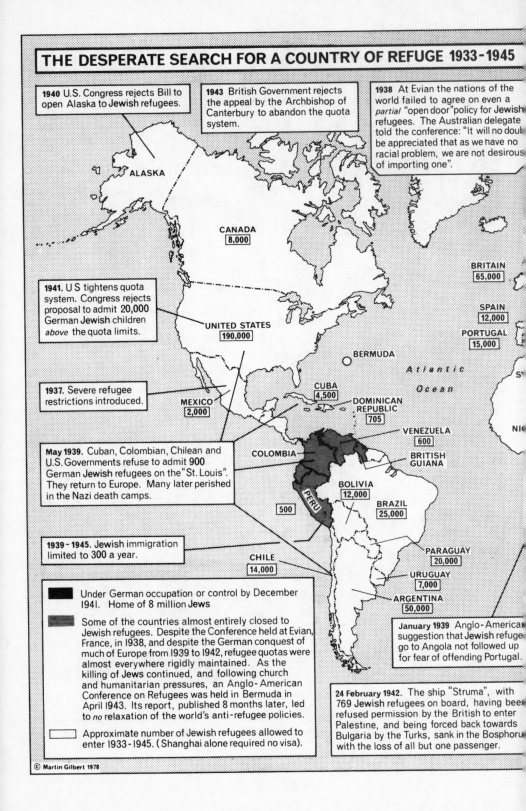

1940 U.S. Congress rejects Bill to open Alaska to Jewish refugees.

1943 British Government rejects the appeal by the Archbishop of Canterbury to abandon the quota system.

1938 At Evian the nations of the world failed to agree on even a *partial* "open door" policy for Jewish refugees. The Australian delegate told the conference: "It will no doubt be appreciated that as we have no racial problem, we are not desirous of importing one".

1941. U S tightens quota system. Congress rejects proposal to admit 20,000 German Jewish children *above* the quota limits.

1937. Severe refugee restrictions introduced.

May 1939. Cuban, Colombian, Chilean and U.S. Governments refuse to admit 900 German Jewish refugees on the "St. Louis". They return to Europe. Many later perished in the Nazi death camps.

1939 - 1945. Jewish immigration limited to 300 a year.

ALASKA

CANADA 8,000

UNITED STATES 190,000

MEXICO 2,000

BERMUDA

CUBA 4,500

DOMINICAN REPUBLIC 705

VENEZUELA 600

COLOMBIA

BRITISH GUIANA

BOLIVIA 12,000

PERU 500

BRAZIL 25,000

CHILE 14,000

PARAGUAY 20,000

URUGUAY 7,000

ARGENTINA 50,000

Atlantic Ocean

BRITAIN 65,000

SPAIN 12,000

PORTUGAL 15,000

NI

Under German occupation or control by December 1941. Home of 8 million Jews

Some of the countries almost entirely closed to Jewish refugees. Despite the Conference held at Evian, France, in 1938, and despite the German conquest of much of Europe from 1939 to 1942, refugee quotas were almost everywhere rigidly maintained. As the killing of Jews continued, and following church and humanitarian pressures, an Anglo-American Conference on Refugees was held in Bermuda in April 1943. Its report, published 8 months later, led to *no* relaxation of the world's anti-refugee policies.

Approximate number of Jewish refugees allowed to enter 1933-1945. (Shanghai alone required no visa).

January 1939 Anglo-American suggestion that Jewish refugees go to Angola not followed up for fear of offending Portugal.

24 February 1942. The ship "Struma", with 769 Jewish refugees on board, having been refused permission by the British to enter Palestine, and being forced back towards Bulgaria by the Turks, sank in the Bosphorus with the loss of all but one passenger.

© Martin Gilbert 1978

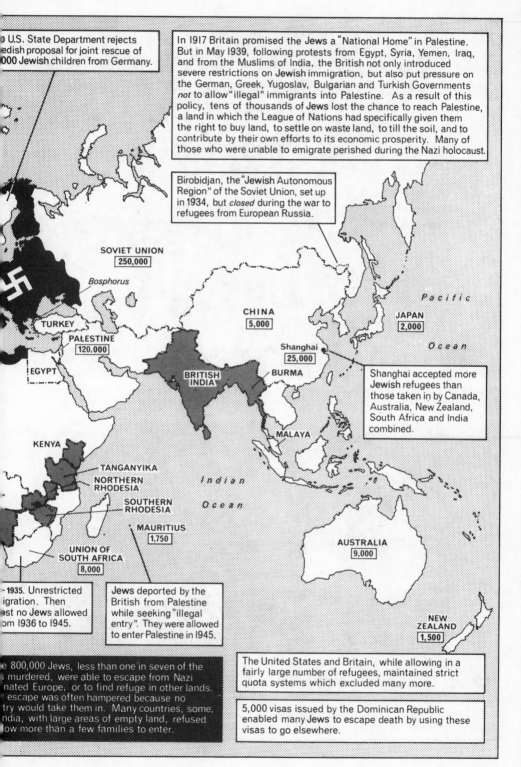

U.S. State Department rejects
[Sw]edish proposal for joint rescue of
[?0]000 Jewish children from Germany.

In 1917 Britain promised the Jews a "National Home" in Palestine.
But in May 1939, following protests from Egypt, Syria, Yemen, Iraq,
and from the Muslims of India, the British not only introduced
severe restrictions on Jewish immigration, but also put pressure on
the German, Greek, Yugoslav, Bulgarian and Turkish Governments
not to allow "illegal" immigrants into Palestine. As a result of this
policy, tens of thousands of Jews lost the chance to reach Palestine,
a land in which the League of Nations had specifically given them
the right to buy land, to settle on waste land, to till the soil, and to
contribute by their own efforts to its economic prosperity. Many of
those who were unable to emigrate perished during the Nazi holocaust.

Birobidjan, the "Jewish Autonomous
Region" of the Soviet Union, set up
in 1934, but *closed* during the war to
refugees from European Russia.

SOVIET UNION
250,000

Bosphorus

Pacific

CHINA
5,000

JAPAN
2,000

Ocean

TURKEY

PALESTINE
120,000

Shanghai
25,000

EGYPT

BRITISH
INDIA

BURMA

Shanghai accepted more
Jewish refugees than
those taken in by Canada,
Australia, New Zealand,
South Africa and India
combined.

MALAYA

KENYA

TANGANYIKA

NORTHERN
RHODESIA

Indian

SOUTHERN
RHODESIA

Ocean

MAURITIUS
1,750

AUSTRALIA
9,000

UNION OF
SOUTH AFRICA
8,000

[19]35. Unrestricted
[imm]igration. Then
[almo]st no Jews allowed
[fr]om 1936 to 1945.

Jews deported by the
British from Palestine
while seeking "illegal
entry". They were allowed
to enter Palestine in 1945.

NEW
ZEALAND
1,500

[Th]e 800,000 Jews, less than one in seven of the
[Jews] murdered, were able to escape from Nazi
[domi]nated Europe, or to find refuge in other lands.
[Their] escape was often hampered because no
[coun]try would take them in. Many countries, some,
[like I]ndia, with large areas of empty land, refused
[to all]ow more than a few families to enter.

The United States and Britain, while allowing in a
fairly large number of refugees, maintained strict
quota systems which excluded many more.

5,000 visas issued by the Dominican Republic
enabled many Jews to escape death by using these
visas to go elsewhere.

Map 12

Plate 29: A sign outside a German village, photographed by a Dutch motor-cyclist in the autumn of 1935. It reads: 'Jews. Attention. The road to Palestine does not go through this locality'.

Plate 30: Jewish refugees from central Europe reach the Black Sea, 1938. Their journey across the Black Sea, the Aegean Sea, and the Eastern Mediterranean was made more perilous by the British Government's attempts to prevent them from reaching Palestine.

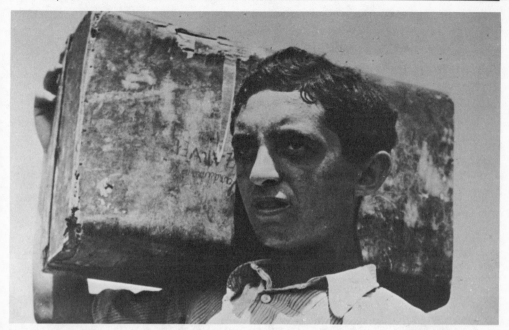

Plate 31: Seventeen year old Moshe Mogilowski, from Jedenitz in Bessarabia, reaches Palestine in 1944. He had managed to escape from a concentration camp in which more than twelve thousand Jews were brutally murdered, or died of starvation, cold and disease. Of the 5,000 Jews of his own home town, less than 100 survived the war.

Plate 32: Palestine, 1944. Jewish refugees from Rumania reach safety, the mark of the yellow star still on their jackets.

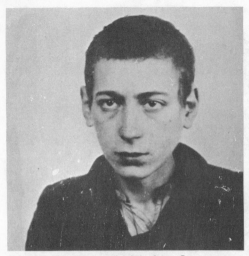

Plate 33: A young Jewish boy from Germany, deported to the Lodz Ghetto.

Plate 34: An Austrian Jew, deported to Lodz.

Plate 35: Belzec extermination camp, a photograph taken in 1946 by a special commission sent to gather the bones of the victims for reburial. The camp operated from May to December 1942, and was designed so that five trainloads, of a thousand people each, could be murdered *in a single day.* In all, 600,000 Jews, and 2,000 non-Jews, were murdered in this one camp. In 1943 the Germans burned all the corpses and scattered their bones.

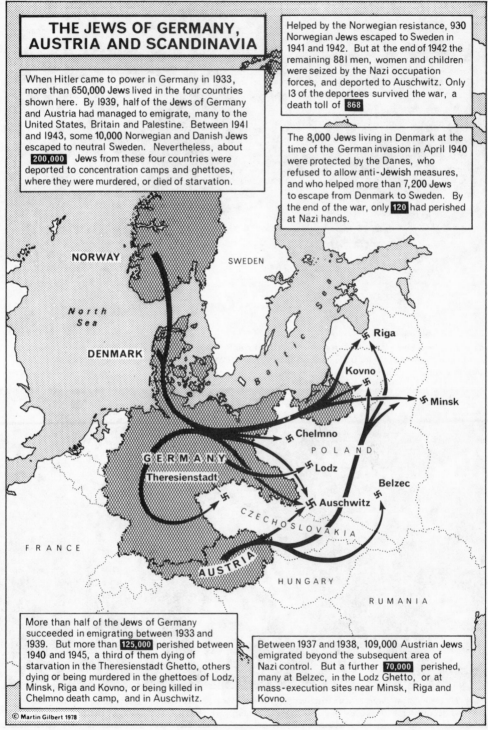

THE JEWS OF GERMANY, AUSTRIA AND SCANDINAVIA

When Hitler came to power in Germany in 1933, more than 650,000 Jews lived in the four countries shown here. By 1939, half of the Jews of Germany and Austria had managed to emigrate, many to the United States, Britain and Palestine. Between 1941 and 1943, some 10,000 Norwegian and Danish Jews escaped to neutral Sweden. Nevertheless, about 200,000 Jews from these four countries were deported to concentration camps and ghettoes, where they were murdered, or died of starvation.

Helped by the Norwegian resistance, 930 Norwegian Jews escaped to Sweden in 1941 and 1942. But at the end of 1942 the remaining 881 men, women and children were seized by the Nazi occupation forces, and deported to Auschwitz. Only 13 of the deportees survived the war, a death toll of 868

The 8,000 Jews living in Denmark at the time of the German invasion in April 1940 were protected by the Danes, who refused to allow anti-Jewish measures, and who helped more than 7,200 Jews to escape from Denmark to Sweden. By the end of the war, only 120 had perished at Nazi hands.

NORWAY

SWEDEN

North Sea

Baltic Sea

DENMARK

Riga

Kovno

Minsk

Chelmno

POLAND

GERMANY

Theresienstadt

Lodz

Belzec

Auschwitz

CZECHOSLOVAKIA

FRANCE

AUSTRIA

HUNGARY

RUMANIA

More than half of the Jews of Germany succeeded in emigrating between 1933 and 1939. But more than 125,000 perished between 1940 and 1945, a third of them dying of starvation in the Theresienstadt Ghetto, others dying or being murdered in the ghettoes of Lodz, Minsk, Riga and Kovno, or being killed in Chelmno death camp, and in Auschwitz.

Between 1937 and 1938, 109,000 Austrian Jews emigrated beyond the subsequent area of Nazi control. But a further 70,000 perished, many at Belzec, in the Lodz Ghetto, or at mass-execution sites near Minsk, Riga and Kovno.

© Martin Gilbert 1978

Plate 36: Jews being deported from a village in Slovakia. The only possessions they could take with them were those that could be loaded on their horse-drawn carts. At Auschwitz, all these possessions were seized by the Nazis.

Plate 37: Hungarian Jews reach Auschwitz. Those photographed here are the women and children selected as 'unfit for work'. By nightfall, most of them had been gassed, and their bodies burnt.

THE JEWS OF CENTRAL EUROPE

Before the outbreak of the second world war, nearly one and a half million Jews lived in the four countries shown on this map. By the end of the war, more than 900,000 of them had been murdered.

The census of 1930 recorded 356,830 Jews in Czechoslovakia. Between 1937 and 1939 some 50,000 emigrated, 12,000 of them going "illegally" to Palestine, where 2,000 of them enlisted in the Allied armies. By 1945, only 30,000 of those who remained were still alive. More than 277,000 had perished, some in Theresienstadt, but most of them at Auschwitz, Maidanek, Treblinka and Sobibor.

Treblinka

Maidanek

Sobibor

Auschwitz

Buchenwald

Theresienstadt

CZECHOSLOVAKIA

TRANSNISTRIA

Dachau

Mauthausen

AUSTRIA

HUNGARY

RUMANIA

YUGOSLAVIA

Jasenovac

Gospić

Sajmište

Black Sea

Adriatic Sea

More than 600,000 Jews lived in Rumania between the wars. Of these, 264,900 were murdered between 1941 and 1944. Many were killed by local Rumanian fascists, who also supervised mass deportations to Transnistria. Thousands of Jews died during these deportations, and tens of thousands died in concentration camps throughout Transnistria.

---- European borders of 1937.

Many Yugoslav Jews were murdered in 1941, in the town and villages where they had lived, by local fascists, and by the German and Hungarian occupation forces. Others were killed between 1941 and 1944 in local concentration camps, or were deported to death camps elsewhere, including Auschwitz, Treblinka, Buchenwald and Dachau. In all, 60,000 Yugoslav Jews perished, nearly 90% of Yugoslav Jewry.

In 1930, 444,567 Jews lived within Hungary's 1920 borders. Of these, at least 300,000 perished between March 1944 and January 1945, more than 95% of them in Auschwitz, where special preparations had been made for gassing up to 10,000 a day, within a few hours of their being sent to the camp by rail from Hungary.

© Martin Gilbert 1978

Plate 38: Mocking a Jew. German soldiers laugh as a Polish Jew is made to put on his prayer shawl, and then to have his hair and beard cut off. Some Jews were made to kneel down in humiliating postures. Others had the Star of David branded on their foreheads. Such 'sport' was common at the time of the German occupation of Poland in September 1939. At the same time, thousands of Jews were tortured and shot: a prelude to the destruction of nearly three million Polish Jews.

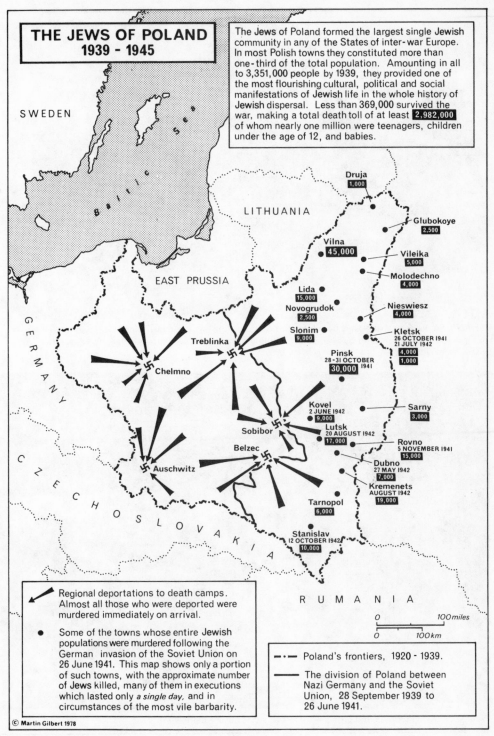

THE JEWS OF POLAND
1939 - 1945

The Jews of Poland formed the largest single Jewish community in any of the States of inter-war Europe. In most Polish towns they constituted more than one-third of the total population. Amounting in all to 3,351,000 people by 1939, they provided one of the most flourishing cultural, political and social manifestations of Jewish life in the whole history of Jewish dispersal. Less than 369,000 survived the war, making a total death toll of at least **2,982,000** of whom nearly one million were teenagers, children under the age of 12, and babies.

SWEDEN

Baltic Sea

LITHUANIA

Druja
1,000

Glubokoye
2,500

Vilna
45,000

Vileika
5,000

EAST PRUSSIA

Molodechno
4,000

Lida
15,000

Novogrudok
2,500

Nieswiesz
4,000

Slonim
9,000

Treblinka

Kletsk
26 OCTOBER 1941
21 JULY 1942
4,000
1,000

GERMANY

Chelmno

Pinsk
28-31 OCTOBER
1941
30,000

Kovel
2 JUNE 1942
9,000

Sarny
3,000

Sobibor

Lutsk
20 AUGUST 1942
17,000

Belzec

Rovno
5 NOVEMBER 1941
15,000

C Z E C H O S L O V A K I A

Auschwitz

Dubno
27 MAY 1942
7,000

Kremenets
AUGUST 1942
19,000

Tarnopol
6,000

Stanislav
12 OCTOBER 1942
10,000

R U M A N I A

Regional deportations to death camps. Almost all those who were deported were murdered immediately on arrival.

Some of the towns whose entire Jewish populations were murdered following the German invasion of the Soviet Union on 26 June 1941. This map shows only a portion of such towns, with the approximate number of Jews killed, many of them in executions which lasted only *a single day,* and in circumstances of the most vile barbarity.

0   100 miles
0   100 km

—·—·— Poland's frontiers, 1920 - 1939.

———— The division of Poland between Nazi Germany and the Soviet Union, 28 September 1939 to 26 June 1941.

© Martin Gilbert 1978

Plate 39: A Jewish mother and her child shot down on the eastern front. More than two and a half million Jews were murdered by special Nazi 'killing squads' who went from village to village, massacring everyone.

Plate 40: Jewish women and girls are forced to strip, before being shot.

THE JEWS OF WESTERN RUSSIA, THE UKRAINE AND THE CRIMEA

0 ___ 150 miles
0 ___ 100 km

Following their invasion of Russia in June 1941, the Germans conquered an area in which more than 2,700,000 Jews were living. Some 250,000 managed to escape eastwards, into unoccupied Russia. But of the remaining 2,450,000, all but 100,000 were murdered, mostly within a few days of the arrival of Nazi and S.S. forces. The massacres at Odessa, Nikolaev, and in Transnistria were carried out largely by the Rumanian occupation forces.

FINLAND

Leningrad

ESTONIA

Baltic Sea

LATVIA

LITHUANIA

Moscow

Polotsk
8,000

Vitebsk
4,090

Smolensk
3,000

Borisov
8,200

Mogilev
4,844

Minsk
21,000

Bobruisk
6,179

Gomel
4,000

U S S R

Warsaw

POLAND

Chernigov
10,000

Kharkov
20,000

Kiev
50,000

Babi Yar
100,000

Poltava
12,000

River Don

Stalingrad

Zhitomir
7,000

UKRAINE

Uman
30,000

Dniepropetrovsk
31,000

Taganrog
2,000

Berdichev
35,000

Mariupol
9,000

Rostov
18,000

Melitopol
2,000

Nikolaev

Essentuki
1,500

Piatigorsk
1,500

River Bug

River Dniester

TRANSNISTRIA
100,000

Kislovodsk
2,000

RUMANIA

Odessa
26,000
60,000

CRIMEA

Kerch
7,000

Simferopol
9,600

Caucasus

Caspian Sea

Bakchiserai
1,099

Black Sea

BULGARIA

---- The western boundary of the Soviet Union in 1937.

▲▲▲ The furthest eastward advance of the German army, 1942.

■ The death-toll in 32 towns. Most of those murdered were shot at mass-extermination sites, forced into buildings and burned alive, or (as in the case of Bakchiserai), driven into the sea and drowned

© Martin Gilbert 1978

This map shows less than one-fifth of the total death toll in western Russia, where more than 2,350,000 Jewish men, women and children were murdered. Some of the "precise" figures, as for Bobruisk or Mogilev, come from German statistics compiled at the very moment of the executions. Many of these figures, as for Simferopol, are for a single day of killing. The death toll for Minsk is that of three separate days of executions all in 1941: one at the end of September, the second on November 6, and the third on November 20. At Smolensk the first to be murdered, in October 1941, were children, old people, and people too sick to do forced labour; then, in February 1942, all women, and all children under 16 were killed; finally on 20 May 1942, all the men were shot.

Map 16

Plate 41: Jews forced to assemble in a narrow ravine near the village of Mizocz, in the Volyn, not far from the town of Kovel. . . .

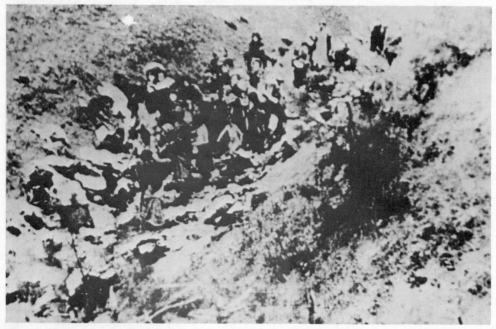

Plate 42: Ordered to undress. . . .

Plate 43: Machine-gunned. . . .

Plate 44: Within a few minutes, a whole Jewish community had been destroyed, and eight centuries of Jewish life and culture obliterated for ever. In most of the mass executions in the Volyn, all able-bodied men were separated from the old, sick, and the children, who were massacred first.

Plate 45: The Warsaw Ghetto uprising. Jewish fighters, captured by the Germans, await their fate.

Plate 46: The Warsaw Ghetto uprising. A Jewish girl fighter is captured in a bunker. During a month of fighting, the Germans killed or deported more than 56,000 Jews. Most of those captured were murdered at Treblinka extermination camp, where more than 370,000 of Warsaw's Jews had already been killed, or murdered in the Ghetto itself.

JEWISH REVOLTS 1942–1945

Despite the overwhelming military strength of the German forces, many Jews, while weakened by hunger and terrorised by Nazi brutality, nevertheless rose in revolt against their fate, not only in many of the Ghettoes in which they were forcibly confined, but even in the concentration camps themselves, snatching from the very gates of death the slender possibility of survival.

✡ Ghettoes in which Jews rose up in revolt against the Germans, with dates. Many of those who revolted were able to escape to the woods, and to join Jewish, Polish or Soviet partisan groups.

卐 Death camps in which the Jews revolted, with date of the revolt. In almost every instance, those who revolted were later caught and murdered.

This map shows twenty of the Ghettoes and five of the death camps in which Jews joined together and sought, often almost unarmed, to strike back at their tormentors. These twenty-five uprisings are among the most noble and courageous episodes not only of Jewish, but of world history.

PONARY
19 MAY 1944

Vilna
1 SEPTEMBER 1943

River Neimen

0   miles   50
0   km   80

Mir
9 AUGUST 1942

Nieswiesz
22 JULY 1942

Kuldichvo
25 MARCH 1943

Kletsk
21 JULY 1943

Bialystok
16 AUGUST 1943

River Vistula

TREBLINKA
2 AUGUST 1943

Lakhva
3 SEPTEMBER 1942

Warsaw
19 APRIL 1943

Minsk Mazowiecki
10 JANUARY 1943

CHELMNO
17 JANUARY 1945

Krushin
17 DECEMBER 1942

SOBIBOR
14 OCTOBER 1943

River Bug

Lublin
3 NOVEMBER 1943

Lutsk
12 OCTOBER 1942

Chenstochov
25 OCTOBER 1943

Bedzin
3 AUGUST 1943

Vistula

River

Tuchin
3 SEPTEMBER 1942

Tarnow
1 SEPTEMBER 1943

Brody
17 MAY 1943

Kremenetz
9 SEPTEMBER 1942

AUSCHWITZ
7 OCTOBER 1944

Lvov
1 JUNE 1943

River

Dniester

Stryj
28 APRIL 1943

C Z E C H O S L O V A K I A

HUNGARY

© Martin Gilbert 1978

42

Map 17

Plate 47: Jewish partisans in France display with pride their defiant emblem, the Star of David.

Plate 48: Jewish partisans enter Vilna at the time of the city's liberation in July 1944. Standing, centre, is the poet Abba Kovner, who subsequently emigrated to Israel.

JEWISH PARTISANS AND RESISTANCE FIGHTERS

This map shows some of the areas in which Jewish resistance fighters were particularly prominent and active in destroying German military stores and communications, and in seizing whole regions from German control.

As well as the Jewish revolts in Ghettoes and Death Camps, many Jews fought in resistance and partisan units throughout Nazi-occupied Europe. Some fought as individuals within local resistance groups, while others formed specifically Jewish units, working closely with local and national underground groups.

FINLAND

SWEDEN
neutral

North Sea

Baltic Sea

SOVIET
Pskov
UNION

GREAT BRITAIN

Berlin
GERMANY
BELGIUM

POLAND

Vilna

Mogilev

Gomel

Koniecpol

NAZI-CONTROLLED EUROPE

SLOVAKIA

Gorodenka

SWITZ.

HUNGARY

FRANCE
Lyons

RUMANIA

Toulouse

YUGOSLAVIA

Black Sea

SPAIN
neutral

ITALY

BULGARIA

GREECE

TURKEY
neutral

0 : miles : 150
0 : km : 100

Mediterranean Sea

FROM PALESTINE

Areas in which specifically Jewish partisan groups attacked and harassed the German occupation forces.

• Thirty-eight of the towns and villages in eastern Europe near which Jewish partisan groups were active in the behind-the-lines struggle against the German occupation forces, attacking German troops, cutting railway lines, and forming focal points for local anti-Nazi resistance. Those who were captured were all tortured and shot. Several thousand Jews also fought in Soviet and Polish partisan units.

➤ Jewish soldiers from Palestine and Britain who were parachuted *behind* enemy lines, in order to link up with resistance groups.

–·–·– European boundaries of 1937.

© Martin Gilbert 1978

44

Map 18

Plate 49: Children at play, Theresienstadt.

Plate 50: Deportation from Theresienstadt.

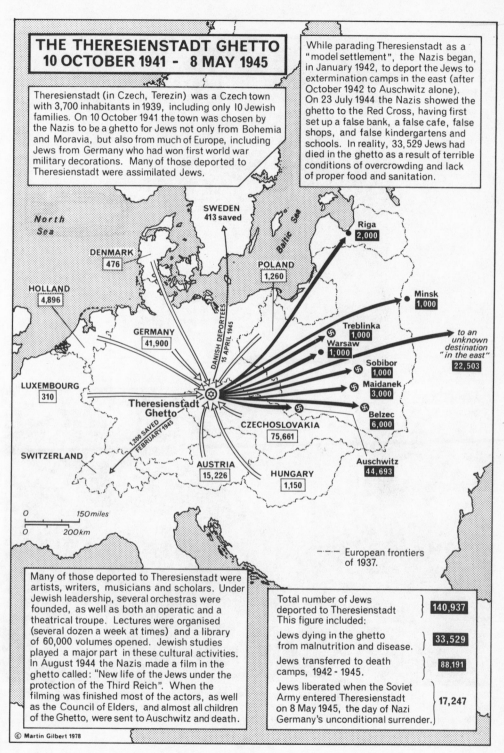

THE THERESIENSTADT GHETTO
10 OCTOBER 1941 - 8 MAY 1945

Theresienstadt (in Czech, Terezin) was a Czech town with 3,700 inhabitants in 1939, including only 10 Jewish families. On 10 October 1941 the town was chosen by the Nazis to be a ghetto for Jews not only from Bohemia and Moravia, but also from much of Europe, including Jews from Germany who had won first world war military decorations. Many of those deported to Theresienstadt were assimilated Jews.

While parading Theresienstadt as a "model settlement", the Nazis began, in January 1942, to deport the Jews to extermination camps in the east (after October 1942 to Auschwitz alone). On 23 July 1944 the Nazis showed the ghetto to the Red Cross, having first set up a false bank, a false cafe, false shops, and false kindergartens and schools. In reality, 33,529 Jews had died in the ghetto as a result of terrible conditions of overcrowding and lack of proper food and sanitation.

North Sea

Baltic Sea

SWEDEN
413 saved

DENMARK
476

POLAND
1,260

HOLLAND
4,896

Riga
2,000

Minsk
1,000

GERMANY
41,900

DANISH DEPORTEES 15 APRIL 1945

Treblinka
1,000

Warsaw
1,000

to an unknown destination "in the east"
22,503

LUXEMBOURG
310

Sobibor
1,000

Maidanek
3,000

Theresienstadt Ghetto

Belzec
6,000

CZECHOSLOVAKIA
75,661

1,200 SAVED FEBRUARY 1945

SWITZERLAND

Auschwitz
44,693

AUSTRIA
15,226

HUNGARY
1,150

0   150 miles
0   200 km

–·–·– European frontiers of 1937.

Many of those deported to Theresienstadt were artists, writers, musicians and scholars. Under Jewish leadership, several orchestras were founded, as well as both an operatic and a theatrical troupe. Lectures were organised (several dozen a week at times) and a library of 60,000 volumes opened. Jewish studies played a major part in these cultural activities. In August 1944 the Nazis made a film in the ghetto called: "New life of the Jews under the protection of the Third Reich". When the filming was finished most of the actors, as well as the Council of Elders, and almost all children of the Ghetto, were sent to Auschwitz and death.

Total number of Jews deported to Theresienstadt This figure included: **140,937**

Jews dying in the ghetto from malnutrition and disease. **33,529**

Jews transferred to death camps, 1942 - 1945. **88,191**

Jews liberated when the Soviet Army entered Theresienstadt on 8 May 1945, the day of Nazi Germany's unconditional surrender. **17,247**

© Martin Gilbert 1978

Plate 51: Anne Frank.

Plate 52: Two Jewish girls liberated near Bergen-Belsen by advancing American troops. Rescue came on 1 May 1945, a week before the end of the war in Europe. In the railway truck behind them are the bodies of those who had died of starvation and disease while being shunted from camp to camp and town to town in the final months of the war.

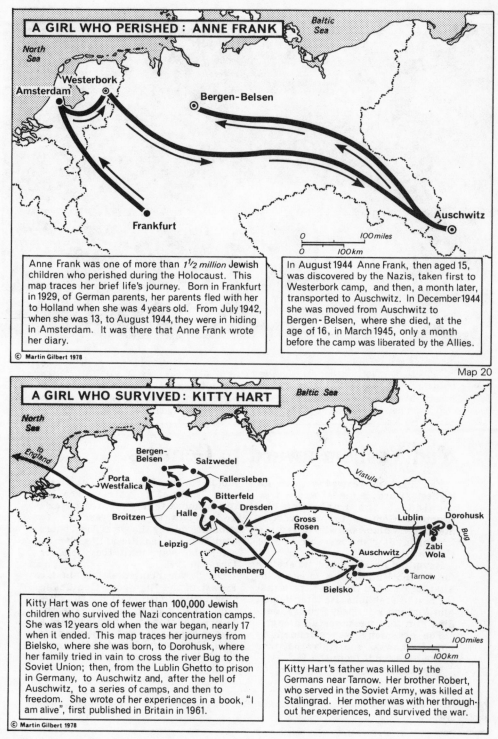

A GIRL WHO PERISHED : ANNE FRANK

Baltic Sea

North Sea

Westerbork

Amsterdam

Bergen-Belsen

Frankfurt

Auschwitz

0   100 miles

0   100 km

Anne Frank was one of more than *1½ million* Jewish children who perished during the Holocaust. This map traces her brief life's journey. Born in Frankfurt in 1929, of German parents, her parents fled with her to Holland when she was 4 years old. From July 1942, when she was 13, to August 1944, they were in hiding in Amsterdam. It was there that Anne Frank wrote her diary.

© Martin Gilbert 1978

In August 1944 Anne Frank, then aged 15, was discovered by the Nazis, taken first to Westerbork camp, and then, a month later, transported to Auschwitz. In December 1944 she was moved from Auschwitz to Bergen-Belsen, where she died, at the age of 16, in March 1945, only a month before the camp was liberated by the Allies.

Map 20

A GIRL WHO SURVIVED : KITTY HART

Baltic Sea

North Sea

to England

Bergen-Belsen

Salzwedel

Porta Westfalica

Fallersleben

Bitterfeld

Broitzen

Halle

Dresden

Gross Rosen

Lublin

Dorohusk

Vistula

Bug

Leipzig

Zabi Wola

Reichenberg

Auschwitz

Tarnow

Bielsko

Kitty Hart was one of fewer than **100,000** Jewish children who survived the Nazi concentration camps. She was 12 years old when the war began, nearly 17 when it ended. This map traces her journeys from Bielsko, where she was born, to Dorohusk, where her family tried in vain to cross the river Bug to the Soviet Union; then, from the Lublin Ghetto to prison in Germany, to Auschwitz and, after the hell of Auschwitz, to a series of camps, and then to freedom. She wrote of her experiences in a book, "I am alive", first published in Britain in 1961.

© Martin Gilbert 1978

0   100 miles

0   100 km

Kitty Hart's father was killed by the Germans near Tarnow. Her brother Robert, who served in the Soviet Army, was killed at Stalingrad. Her mother was with her throughout her experiences, and survived the war.

Map 21

Plate 53: In this house, in a town in southern Poland, a Polish mechanic, Józef Zwonarz, hid a Jewish family throughout the German occupation, and looked after them, despite the death-penalty had he been caught. Both he and the Jews he sheltered survived. This photograph was taken in 1964.

Yad Vashem award to Gentiles

Yad Vashem yesterday gave its highest award, a medal and a tree planted in the Forest of the Righteous Gentiles, to the Reverend Stanislaw Falkowski who saved the life of a Jewish boy during the Holocaust.

Reverend Falkowski found shelter for Joseph Kutrzeba, a 15-year-old, after he escaped from the train taking him to Treblinka. He later helped him find work in East Prussia, sending him food packages all along.

The ceremony was attended by both Falkowski and Kutrzeba, who came here for it from the U.S.

The award will also be given on Sunday to Dr. Hadji Mitkov and Pandora Todor of Yugoslavia who hid the Frances family from the Nazis and arranged their escape to Albania, during the war. The Todors also fed and sheltered the family after the war, until they left for Israel in 1948.

Dr. Todor planted a tree in the Forest of the Righteous Gentiles in 1962 during a visit to Israel. His wife, now visiting here, will receive the Yad Vashem medal and also plant a tree in honour of her brother and his wife, Trajko and Dragica Ribarew, for their part in helping the Frances family.

Plate 54: A news item, published in the *Jerusalem Post* on 4 November 1977. Similar items appear almost every week.

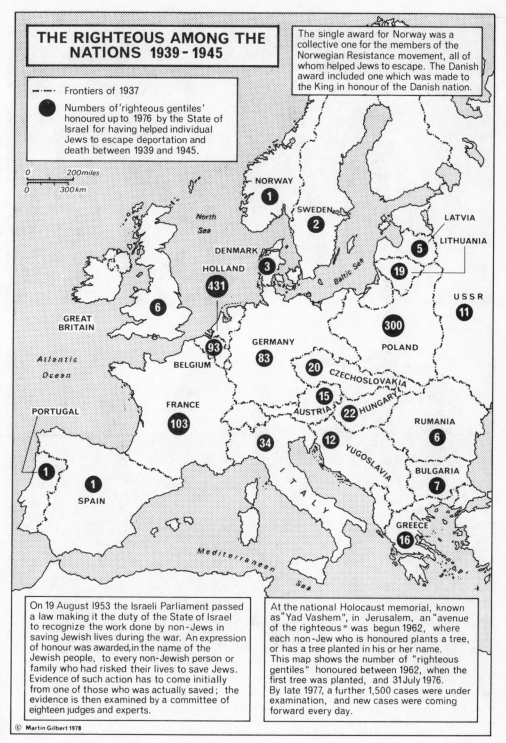

THE RIGHTEOUS AMONG THE NATIONS 1939-1945

The single award for Norway was a collective one for the members of the Norwegian Resistance movement, all of whom helped Jews to escape. The Danish award included one which was made to the King in honour of the Danish nation.

–·–·– Frontiers of 1937

⬤ Numbers of 'righteous gentiles' honoured up to 1976 by the State of Israel for having helped individual Jews to escape deportation and death between 1939 and 1945.

0   200miles
0   300km

NORWAY **1**

SWEDEN **2**

LATVIA

LITHUANIA

5

DENMARK **3**

HOLLAND **431**

North Sea

Baltic Sea

19

USSR **11**

GREAT BRITAIN **6**

BELGIUM **93**

GERMANY **83**

POLAND **300**

20 CZECHOSLOVAKIA

15 AUSTRIA

22 HUNGARY

RUMANIA **6**

Atlantic Ocean

FRANCE **103**

PORTUGAL **1**

SPAIN **1**

34

ITALY

12 YUGOSLAVIA

BULGARIA **7**

GREECE **16**

Mediterranean Sea

On 19 August 1953 the Israeli Parliament passed a law making it the duty of the State of Israel to recognize the work done by non-Jews in saving Jewish lives during the war. An expression of honour was awarded, in the name of the Jewish people, to every non-Jewish person or family who had risked their lives to save Jews. Evidence of such action has to come initially from one of those who was actually saved; the evidence is then examined by a committee of eighteen judges and experts.

At the national Holocaust memorial, known as "Yad Vashem", in Jerusalem, an "avenue of the righteous" was begun 1962, where each non-Jew who is honoured plants a tree, or has a tree planted in his or her name. This map shows the number of "righteous gentiles" honoured between 1962, when the first tree was planted, and 31 July 1976. By late 1977, a further 1,500 cases were under examination, and new cases were coming forward every day.

© Martin Gilbert 1978

Plate 55: Four Jewish men and a boy about to be shot at Sniadowa, a village near to the Polish town of Lomza.

Plate 56: After the war, unveiling a memorial to the 60,000 Berlin Jews who were murdered during the Second World War.

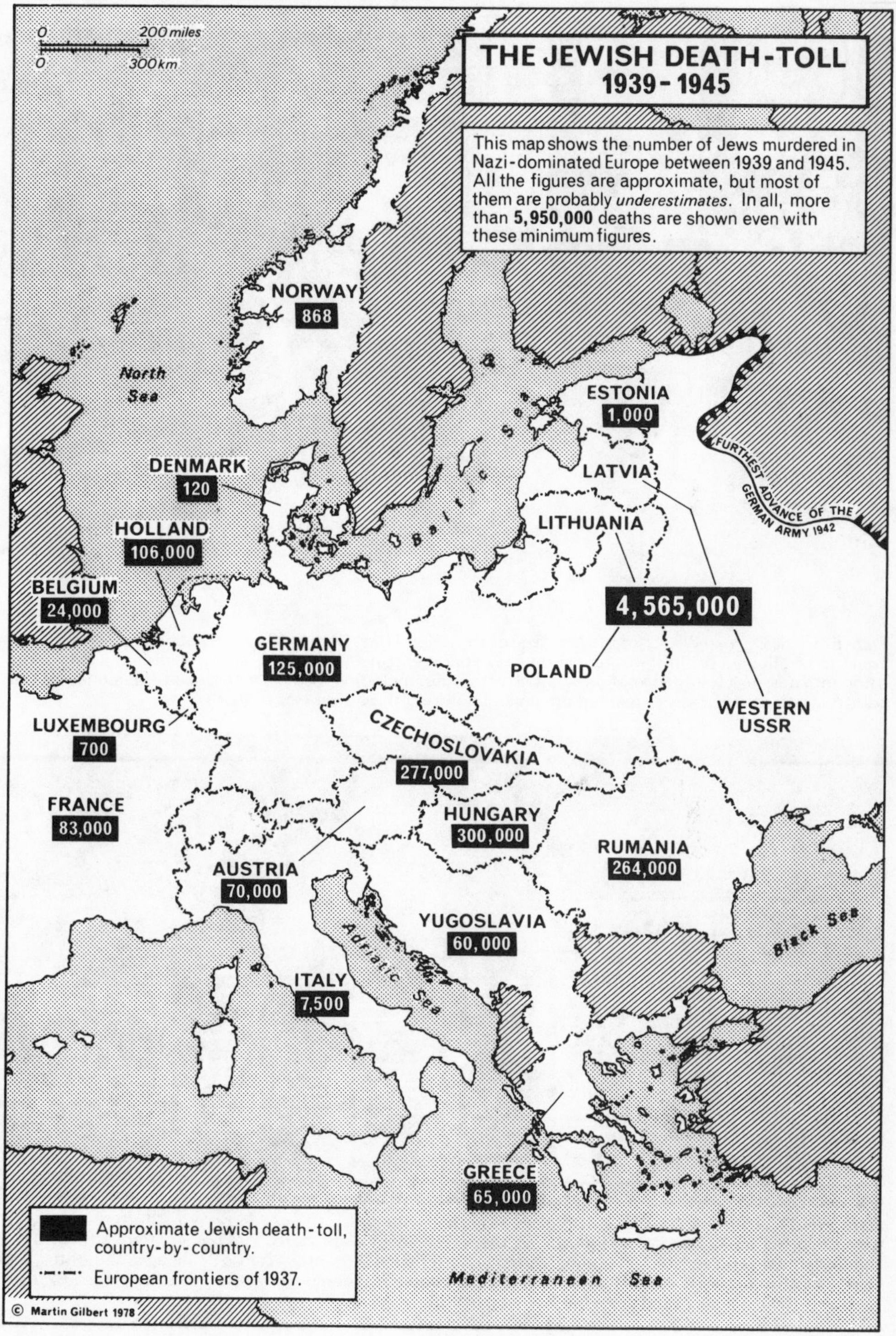
THE JEWISH DEATH-TOLL 1939-1945
This map shows the number of Jews murdered in Nazi-dominated Europe between 1939 and 1945. All the figures are approximate, but most of them are probably *underestimates*. In all, more than **5,950,000** deaths are shown even with these minimum figures.
0 200 miles
0 300 km
NORWAY 868
North Sea
DENMARK 120
HOLLAND 106,000
BELGIUM 24,000
LUXEMBOURG 700
FRANCE 83,000
GERMANY 125,000
ESTONIA 1,000
LATVIA
LITHUANIA
4,565,000
POLAND
WESTERN USSR
FURTHEST ADVANCE OF THE GERMAN ARMY 1942
Baltic Sea
CZECHOSLOVAKIA 277,000
HUNGARY 300,000
AUSTRIA 70,000
RUMANIA 264,000
YUGOSLAVIA 60,000
ITALY 7,500
Adriatic Sea
Black Sea
GREECE 65,000
Mediterranean Sea
Approximate Jewish death-toll, country-by-country.
European frontiers of 1937.
© Martin Gilbert 1978

Plate 57: The Dachau War Crimes trials. One of the defendants, Doctor Klaus Karl Schilling, appeals to the court to be allowed to finish his report on the experiments he had carried out on Jewish concentration camp inmates. Much evidence of anti-Jewish atrocities, including medical experiments which led to the painful death of those experimented on, emerged during these post-war trials.

Plate 58: The memorial to the Jewish dead of a single Hungarian town, Fászberésy. All those named here were deported to Auschwitz, and murdered there. The memorial records 224 names, among them sixteen children under ten years old, including Zsuzsi Schäffer aged 3 months, Tamas Schik aged 9 months, and Gyurika Sztrimber aged 7 months. Among the old people murdered were Istvanne Spitzer aged 82, Hermann Klein aged 87, and Jozsefne Reiner aged 88.

A NOTE ON SOURCES

In preparing the maps themselves, I made use of a wide variety of sources, including the multi-volume *Yad Vashem Studies on the European Jewish Catastrophe and Resistance,* the first volume of which was published in Jerusalem in 1957. These volumes continue to appear at regular intervals. One of the first publications to include captured war-time documents of the Holocaust period was *The Black Book: The Nazi Crime Against The Jewish People,* published in New York in 1946 by the Jewish Black Book Committee. The longest single published documentary source so far for the Holocaust is the forty-two volume *Trial of the Major War Criminals Before The International Military Tribunal: Official Text,* published in Nuremberg between 1947 and 1949. These volumes were followed between 1949 and 1953 by a further fifteen volumes, *Trials of War Criminals Before the Nuremberg Military Tribunals Under Control Council Law No. 10,* published in Washington, D.C. Both these sets of Trials draw upon, and reproduce in their entirety, a vast mass of original documents, on the basis of which several thousand maps could be drawn, without exhausting either the territorial range or the factual details of Nazi terror.

The numbers shown in the Atlas of those who died — Jew and non-Jew alike — were taken from a wide variety of sources. While the war was still being fought the Germans themselves compiled detailed lists of transports and exterminations. Many of these lists survived, and were captured by the Allied forces at the time of the liberation. So too did the diary of the Commandant of Auschwitz. These documents can be found in the Nuremberg volumes cited above, and in the many specialist works researched and produced since the war. Further evidence of the numbers of those who were murdered has been compiled by comparing the numbers of post-war survivors with the pre-war census lists for almost all the European countries. There is full confirmation of these figures in the evidence produced at the thousands of anti-Nazi trials which began in 1945: trials which continue to this day in the countries formerly under Nazi rule. Further confirmation is being published each year in the researches of historians in several countries into the many community archives and local records which have survived. A detailed account of the materials available on these figures is given in the book *Six Million Did Die,* by Arthur Suzman and Denis Diamond.

A comprehensive study of many of the communities destroyed in the Holocaust can be found in the sixteen-volume *Encyclopaedia Judaica,* Jerusalem 1971, where the many country-by-country and town-by-town entries give a graphic introduction to the scale and nature of the Holocaust: each entry includes its own source list, while the 44-page entry for the Holocaust is itself a substantial one, and contains a comprehensive bibliography.

LIST OF SOURCES FOR THE ILLUSTRATIONS

Dr. A. Ben Bernfes: Plates 20, 21

Jack Bruckenstein: Plate 15

Contact, Amsterdam: Plate 51

The Jerusalem Post: Plate 54

The Jewish National and University Library, Jerusalem: Plate 8

Keren Hayesod Information Department Photo Archives: Plate 31, 32

George Loukomski, *Jewish Art in European Synagogues,* London 1947:
    Plates 3, 4, 5

The Orient Press Photo Company, Photo Z. Kluger: Plate 59

Franz Preissler: Plate 16

Jacob J. Rutstein: Plate 13

United States Army, Service Corps Photograph: Plates 19, 52, 57

Yad Vashem, Jerusalem: Plates 2, 6, 7, 10, 12, 14, 17, 18, 24, 30, 33, 34,
    35, 36, 38, 40, 41, 42, 43, 44, 45, 46, 47, 48, 49, 50, 55, 56, 58

H. Roger Viollet, Paris; printed in Abba Eban, *My People,* New York, 1938:
    Plate 9

The Wiener Library, London: Plates 1, 11, 22, 23, 25, 26, 27, 28, 29, 37, 39

Zydowski Instytut Historyczny, Warsaw: Plate 53

READING LIST

Reuben Ainsztein, *Jewish Resistance in Nazi-Occupied Eastern Europe* (Barnes and Noble Books)

Allan Bullock, *Hitler: A Study in Tyranny* (Bantam Books)

Lucy S. Dawidowicz, *A Holocaust Reader* (Behrman House)

The Diary of Anne Frank (Doubleday)

Martin Gilbert, *Exile and Return* (Lippincott)

Jacob Glatstein, and others, *Anthology of Holocaust Literature* (Atheneum)

Kitty Hart, *I Am Alive* (Corgi Books)

Gideon Hausner, *Justice in Jerusalem* (Harper & Row)

Raul Hilberg, *The Destruction of the European Jews* (New Viewpoints)

Abraham I. Katsch, *The Warsaw Diary of Chaim A. Kaplan* (Collier Books)

Ber Mark, *Uprising in the Warsaw Ghetto* (Schocken Books)

Gerald Reitlinger, *The Final Solution* (A. S. Barnes)

Marie Syrkin, *Blessed Is the Match* (Jewish Publication Society of America)

Elie Wiesel, *Night* (Avon Books)

David W. Zisenwine, *Anti-Semitism in Europe* (Behrman House)

Plate 59: Liberation. Italian Jewish children led by a Jewish soldier of the Jewish Brigade of the British Army. More than 7,750 Italian Jews were deported to Auschwitz and murdered, but more than 25,000 escaped into Switzerland, or found shelter in Italy itself, with peasants, townsfolk and in Catholic religious institutions, all of whom risked heavy penalties for giving such help.

EPILOGUE

This poem was written thirty years after The Holocaust, by one of the survivors, Michael Etkind, who was then a teenager.

BE STRONG

Time: April, nineteen forty five AD
Columns of men — bound east
Place: German Reich — the Third
            designed to last
a thousand years, at least

Strange sight even in the time of war,
            never seen since,
            and never seen before

Exhausted men,
striped suits, striped caps,
            and clog clad feet,
            dragging through mud,
            through rain,
            and penetrating sleet
Keep up — You
remnants of a decimated race
Keep up your strength, and hear:—
The Fuhrer's Dream, Your End,
will soon be over;
and, as it has begun
so will it — disappear

The last convulsions of a dying beast
            can kill
            So you — beware
            You came so far, —
            go on —
            you're nearly there

Pitiless soldiers marching —
            at your side,
            guns pointing
            at the ready
            Go on — march — head down
            eyes straight,
and keep your progress steady

Don't drop behind — don't trip,
don't stagger, — and do not fall;
            don't weaken —
            and do not think
            No — not at all

When shouts and shots you hear —
            ignore them —
            go deaf and dumb
Stifle your mouth, — muffle your ear
            Go on;
            do not succumb —
            the end is near

So long as you can feel
            the cold —
            the wet —
            the hunger,
            and the lice —
            which itch,
            and drink your blood
            You are alive —
            Rejoice
            You will survive
            Be strong,
            it can't be long.